BODY BATTLES

by Rita Golden Gelman

pictures by
Elroy Freem

SCHOLASTIC INC.
New York Toronto London Auckland Sydney

Ta daaaaaa!
Presenting a blood-and-guts
true-to-life thriller about the battles
that go on inside the human body.

ISBN 0-590-44973-7

Text copyright © 1992 by Rita Golden Gelman.
Illustrations copyright © 1992 by Mark Teague.
All rights reserved. Published by Scholastic Inc.

12 11 10 9 8 7 6 5 4 3 2   2 3 4 5 6 7/9

Printed in the U.S.A.   08

First Scholastic printing, April 1992

Dedicated with love and thanks
   to those incredible white blood cells,
   to earwax,
   to stomach acid,
   to the human brain,
   and last but not least,
   to skin.
Let's hear it for skin!

Your body's fantastic.
 It breathes and bends
and jumps and climbs.
 It eats. It sleeps. It laughs.
 That's because inside of you are
trillions of microscopic cells
 hanging out,
 sending messages to each other,
 snacking on vitamins,
 multiplying…
  and killing any bad guys
  that might mess up the works.

It's a
super-sensational,
what-a-creational,
brilliant
and fabulous
body.

Here are the bad guys that might
mess up the works.

VIRUSES and BACTERIA

Viruses and bacteria are microscopic
living things. Some people call them germs.

They stuff your nose,
sore your throat,
fever your body,
itch your skin,
upset your stomach,
water your eyes,
and cause a lot of trouble.
That's why your body tries to
keep them out. It has a whole bunch
of defensive weapons to do the job.

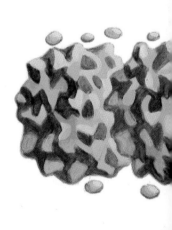

Defensive body weapon number one:

SKIN

Everyone knows that skin keeps your insides from getting out. It also keeps the outside from getting in. Your body is completely wrapped in skin

Skin is tough.
You can pull it and scrub it.
Bend it and wrinkle it.
Walk on it.
Sit on it.
Float it.
And sink it.

It's a
super-sensational,
what-a-creational,
squashable
washable
skin.

Your skin is only one way that your body stops viruses and bacteria from getting in.
Sometimes viruses and bacteria zoom through the air in sneezes and coughs.
And if you're close to the sneezer, you might breathe them in.
That's when you need defensive body weapons number two and number three:

MUCUS AND CILIA

The special skin that lines your breathing tube —
from your nose to your lungs — is wet and slimy
with gluey stuff called mucus.

If you happen to inhale viruses and bacteria,
dust or dirt, they get trapped in the mucus.
Then millions of microscopic hairs
called cilia wave and push the mucus
up and out of the tube.

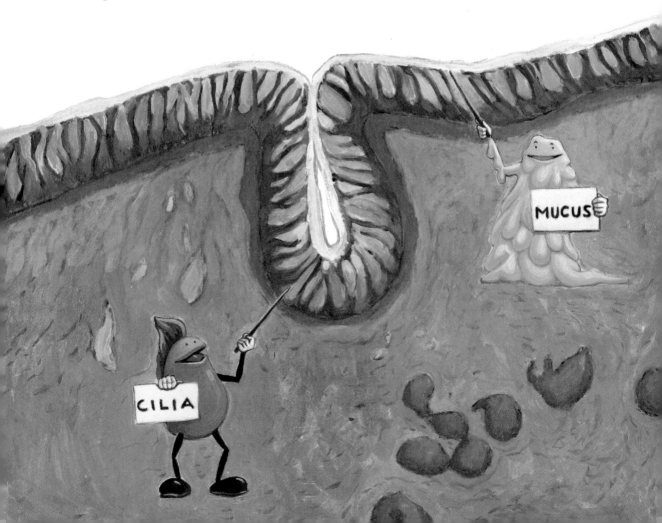

Ears are another way the bad guys can sneak inside.
Defensive body weapon number four is:

EARWAX

Earwax is like mucus, but thicker
and not so slimy. Things like dust and dirt
and tiny insects that fly into your ears
get trapped in the yellow mush...
before they can hurt your hearing.

Ears are amazing,
The noises they hear —
Noises from distances,
Noises from near.

Crickets and thunderstorms,
Sirens and fiddles.
Let's hear it for ears —
inners,
outers,
and middles!

EARWAX

A lot of good stuff gets in
through your mouth,
like peaches and salad, pizza and soup.
But the mouth is an easy entry
for the bad guys as well.

Bacteria and viruses are all over the place.
They live on the skins of unwashed fruit.
They grow on uncooked meats and vegetables.
And millions of them hide out on dirty fingers.
Sometimes they find their way
into your mouth and down to your stomach.

But there's a surprise waiting for them.
Defensive body weapon number five:

STOMACH ACID

Stomach acid is also called
hydrochloric acid or HCl.
It is a powerful acid
that's made in your stomach.
When bacteria and viruses
get into your stomach, they're usually
destroyed,
zapped,
done in by hydrochloric acid.
It's a
super-sensational,
what-a-creational,
deadly and dangerous
stomach…
if you happen to be a germ.

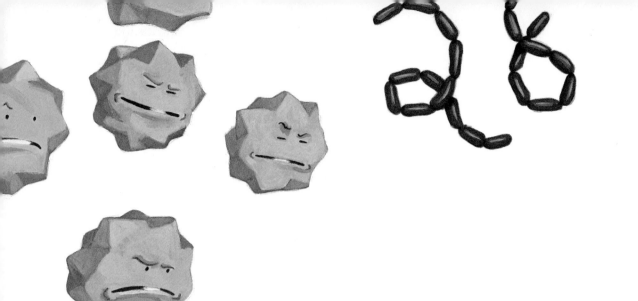

Skin. Mucus. Cilia. Earwax. Stomach acid.
They do a terrific job! But sometimes,
the bad guys get through the skin,
or past the mucus. And sometimes
they survive the stomach…
and wander inside you, looking for a home.
   For viruses and bacteria, a good home
is one that's warm and wet and comfortable —
a place where there's plenty of food.
   The inside of your body is warm.
   It's wonderfully wet. And *you* are the food.

But don't get scared. Your body
knows exactly what's happening.
An alarm goes out: AN ENEMY HAS ENTERED.
And your body turns on
defensive body weapon number six:

THE IMMUNE SYSTEM

The immune system is the body's army. The soldiers are called lymphocytes or white blood cells.

Usually there are a few trillion lymphocyte soldiers just floating around in your body.

But when viruses and bacteria start to cause trouble like colds, or infections, or stomachaches, those lymphocytes go to work.

First the lymphocytes split in two,
making the army twice as big.
And then they split again
and again and again.
   And soon, there are trillions
and trillions of lymphocytes
zapping and popping
and poisoning and gobbling the enemy.
   And making you better.
   Sometimes your body needs
a little help from medicines
that the doctor gives you.
But most of the time,
your body's lymphocytes
get rid of the enemy
all by themselves.
   They're
      super-sensational,
      what-a-creational,
      fearless and
      fabulous
      cells.

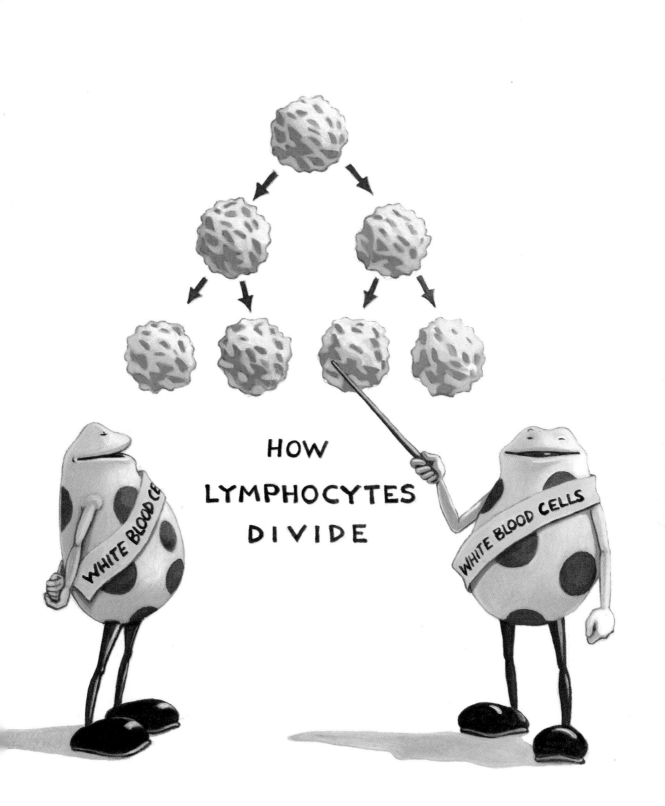

You really have an amazing body.
But you have to help it stay healthy.
    Run it.
    Swim it.
    School it.
    Play it.
    Feed it.
    Sleep it.
    Wash it.
    Weigh it.
And always protect it from
poisons and drugs.

Poisons and drugs are not viruses
  or bacteria. They are chemicals.
  The mucus can't trap them,
  the acid can't zap them,
  the lymphocytes can't kill them,
  and the skin can't always keep them out.
Poisons and drugs can
  stop your breathing,
  mess up your thinking,
  and destroy some very important cells.
Poisons and drugs can kill you.

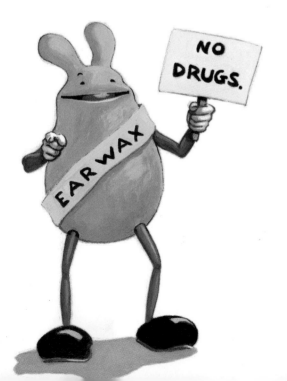

POISONS

They glue wood,
  scrub tubs,
  feed plants,
  clean clothes,
  clear drains,
  wash windows,
  kill bugs,
  paint walls.
  Poisons can be useful around the house.
But they don't belong in your body.
They can make you very sick.

DRUGS

Drugs can mess up your body, too.
People swallow them,
   sniff them,
   smoke them.
And sometimes they inject them
into their blood with a needle.

People who take drugs are sick.
They need help. And their bodies can't
help them. When people take drugs,
their super-sensational,
what-a-creational,
brilliant and
fabulous bodies are
confused,
bewildered,
betrayed.

But you don't have to worry.
Because to keep drugs out of your body,
you have the most powerful defensive
weapon of all.
Defensive body weapon number seven:

THE BRAIN

Your brain lets you think for yourself.
It helps you make decisions.
It gives you the knowledge to stay away
from poisons and the courage to say no
if someone offers you drugs.

Your brain controls
   how you feel,
   how you think,
   how you act.
Your brain controls everything you do.
It gives you the strength and the power
to be you.
   It's a
      super-sensational,
      what-a-creational,
      brilliant
      and trustworthy
      brain.

LET'S HEAR IT FOR THE BODY!

Bodies are fantastic.
Everybody's blood is red.
Everybody has a head.

Hearts pump.
Ears hear.
Skin sweats.
Eyes tear.

Teeth chew.
Tongues talk.
Knees bend.
Legs walk.

Fingers feel.
Nails grow.
Brains think.
Noses blow.

Throats yawn.
Toes wiggle.
Stomachs growl.

People GIGGLE.

BODY BULLE

If you get a cut in your skin, be sure to wash it with soap. And keep it clean.

Stay away from other people's coughs and sneezes.
And cover up your own.

Don't ever stick anything into your ears.
They are very sensitive.

The AIDS virus, called HIV, stops the immune system from building its army. Without its army, the body can't kill the AIDS virus. That's why scientists are looking for ways to kill it with medicine. AIDS is a serious illness; but you *can't* get AIDS from touching someone who has it.

Don't ever eat or drink anything that isn't food. It might be a poison or a drug. There are lots of different kinds of drugs. Some of them look like candy. If you aren't sure, ask someone you trust if it's safe.

Medicines are drugs that you buy in a drugstore. It would probably be less confusing if drugstores were called medicine stores.

Your brain is the most complicated and smartest machine ever made.

It gives you good advice. Listen to it and it will help you stay healthy.

Running and jumping and climbing and biking help keep your body strong. Laughing is also good for your body.

Your body is a glorious, brilliant machine.
Feed it well and keep it clean.
Take care of that body, whatever you do.
'Cause you're a SENSATIONAL FABULOUS YOU!